I0845603

Smart Cities

Combining Technology and Sustainability

Table of Contents

Chapter 1. Introduction

In this special report, we delve into the fascinating interplay between technology and sustainability in the development of Smart Cities. Picture a world where everyday urban living is enhanced with the efficiency of cutting-edge technology hand-in-hand with green, sustainable practices. It may seem complicated, but don't worry! We have unraveled this complex mesh by breaking it down into digestible aspects, giving you a comprehensive yet user-friendly insight into how our future cities could function efficiently, sustainably, and smartly. This report sways away from daunting technical jargon, instead, comfortably navigating you through the exciting advancements and compelling concepts. Brace yourselves for an intriguing journey—the cities of tomorrow await you! Let the lure of understanding how we can build an environmentally conscious, technologically advanced future motivate you to dive into this special report.

Chapter 2. Understanding Smart Cities: An Introduction

The intricate interplay between technology, sustainability, and urban development forms the basis of the evolution of smart cities. Imagine these cities as giant, living laboratories of innovation, where the Internet of Things (IoT), artificial intelligence (AI), and green technologies fuse to create urban environments that are efficient, environmentally friendly, and sublimely interactive.

2.1. Defining Smart Cities

A smart city fuses technology with urban infrastructure to enhance the quality of living of its inhabitants. Leveraging the framework of digitalization, IoT, AI, and Big Data analytics, this urban archetype aims to facilitate streamlined governance, sustainable development, and improved public welfare.

In a smart city, every constituent factor, from transportation and buildings to utilities and services, is integrated into a coherent, interconnected network. Internet connectivity and cloud platforms enable seamless interaction among these elements, thereby enhancing the proficiency of urban systems and services.

To elaborate, let's explore various components of a smart city.

2.2. Technologies Powering Smart Cities

The integration of digital technology into urban infrastructure and living broadens the realm of possibilities for modern cities. Below are a few key technologies underpinning smart cities.

-. **Internet of Things (IoT)**: This involves a network of devices, vehicles, appliances, and other items embedded with sensors, software, and connectivity, allowing them to collect and exchange data.

-. **Artificial Intelligence (AI)**: AI enables the processing of this massive data to derive useful insights, predict trends, and drive intelligent automation.

-. **Big Data Analytics**: This involves the examination of large and varied data sets to uncover patterns, correlations, and trends.

-. **Blockchain**: This technology promises secure transactions, identity verification, and even voting systems.

Providing not just efficient solutions, these technologies collectively help in reducing the environmental footprint.

2.3. Sustainable Practices in Smart Cities

Smart cities envisage an ecologically balanced framework where sustainable practices mitigate the adverse environmental impacts of urbanization. Key focus areas include:

-. **Energy Conservation**: Smart grids, energy-efficient buildings, and renewable energy sources play a key role in reducing energy consumption.

-. **Waste Management**: Advanced waste collection and processing systems aid in effective waste management while promoting recycling.

-. **Green Spaces**: Urban planning involves dedicated green spaces that aid in maintaining biological diversity and improving the city's air quality.

-. **Water Management**: Smart systems are utilized for optimum water usage and conservation, reducing the demand on water sources.

2.4. Benefits of Smart Cities

The notion of smart cities yields several benefits, key among them being:

-. **Improved Quality of Life**: Integrated services, smart mobility solutions, efficient utility services, and IT-backed healthcare considerably enhance living standards.

-. **Sustainable Development**: Smart cities counter environmental degradation with ecologically sensitive solutions that promote sustainability.

-. **Economic Efficiency**: New business models and employment opportunities arise from the digital economy of smart cities.

-. **Enhanced Governance**: The cogent use of digital technology provides governments with essential tools for streamlined, transparent, and efficient administration.

Fostering inclusivity, sustainability, and liveability, smart cities aren't a distant dream anymore. They are anticipated to be a panacea for many urban challenges, including population growth, environmental degradation, resource scarcity, and growing energy demands. Smart cities have embarked on a transformative journey to create a harmonious co-existence of technology and nature, thereby making room for a sustainable future. This remarkable blend not only holds great promise for a comfortable lifestyle but also for a sustainable living space for the generations to come.

We have only scratched the surface of the immense potential that smart cities have to offer. Their complete realization is possibly one of the most exciting prospects of the 21st century. The journey to understanding smart cities must move on. Next, we'll look at the challenges and solutions for building these technologically advanced, yet environmentally conscious cities and much more.

Chapter 3. Building Blocks of Smart Cities

As we commence our exploration of future cities, our starting point will be an intricate look at the foundational pillars that enable urban areas to be tagged as 'smart'. These are the building blocks charged with transforming regular cities into environments where technology and sustainability converge to afford improved and efficient living. Fittingly labeled 'Smart Cities', these urban areas are projected to be the benchmark for future developments.

The cornerstones upon which Smart Cities are built are expansive, encompassing everything from Artificial Intelligence, Internet of Things (IoT), Big Data, Cloud Computing, Sustainable Energy, and Green Architecture. These diverse components collaborate to design urban living within the parameters of intelligence, productivity, sustainability, and community engagement.

3.1. The Role of Artificial Intelligence

Artificial Intelligence (AI) serves as a pivotal building block of Smart Cities, ingrained into an incredibly vast array of urban functionalities. From predictive police operations, traffic management, to waste management and energy consumption optimization—AI's capabilities are pervasive and far-reaching. The operative function of AI in Smart Cities revolves around processing large and diverse sets of data to make predictive analyses, and in turn, yield informed decision-making.

What would that mean for the average resident? Essentially, AI's predictive potential could notify citizens about potential traffic congestion so that they could take an alternative route, alert about eminent harsh weather conditions, or even predict power shortages and redirect energy from higher supply areas.

3.2. Internet of Things: The Interconnected City System

IoT is perhaps the most essential building block of a Smart City. Look at it as a vast interconnected system where data is gathered, shared, and analyzed to enhance urban living. Billions of sensors and devices are scattered across the city infrastructure—on roads, buildings, pipes, power lines—to gather data in real-time. This data is then used to manage resources, detect irregularities, and originate solutions in real-time.

For example, sensors on water pipelines could detect leaks promptly to prevent significant water wastage. Similarly, waste bins equipped with sensors could indicate when they are full, ensuring efficient waste collections and optimum management. Besides, smart meters could provide homeowners with insights about their electricity or gas consumption patterns, allowing for better energy management.

3.3. Harnessing Power from Data: Big Data and Cloud Computing

Big Data's influence is fundamental in any Smart City's dynamics. It is the enormous volumes of data consistently generated by citizens, devices (within the IoT network), and systems which, when effectively managed and interpreted, has the potential to streamline urban living. Coupled with Cloud Computing, this data is stored, analyzed, and accessed over the Internet, delivering a scalable and economical solution for city management.

Big Data and Cloud Computing combined can reduce traffic congestion by offering real-time traffic updates, increase energy efficiency by analyzing consumption patterns, and enhance public safety through crime mapping and predictive policing. The potential with these technologies is limitless.

3.4. Sustainable Energy and Green Architecture: The Green Shift

Eco-friendly and sustainable initiatives are integral to Smart City frameworks. Renewable energy sources, efficient waste disposal systems, green buildings, and sustainable transport models are some prominent aspects of this shift. Smart grids facilitate electricity supply from renewable sources, lowering carbon emissions and promoting energy efficiency. Construction of buildings in a Smart City would employ energy-efficient materials and design, promoting Green Architecture.

Green Architecture not just considers the building's design and construction but also its operation, maintenance, and demolition—aiming to create a minimal carbon footprint. This implies using solar panels, green roofs, rainwater harvesting systems, effective insulation, and more—all working to establish a greener and more sustainable urban environment.

3.5. The Aspect of Community Engagement

A Smart City also empowers its citizens by promoting engagement and participation. Governments are now able to provide e-services through digital platforms, increasing transparency and convenience for citizen-government interactions. For instance, a complaint about a broken streetlight could be filed through a mobile app, speeding up the troubleshooting process.

In the nutshell, these building blocks of Smart Cities function in unison to create an environment where innovation thrives, sustainability is prioritized, and the living standard of citizens is enhanced. Each building block is interdependent, each as vital as the other, working in sync to build a city that is not just smart in name but in functionality and practice, paving the way for a greener, more sustainable future.

Chapter 4. The Role of IoT in Urban Development

The Internet of Things (IoT), a revolutionary technology, works as the central nervous system of Smart Cities, connecting various city elements to enhance urban development. By leveraging a network of sensors and devices, the IoT revolutionizes urban living, addressing sustainability challenges while providing cutting-edge services personally, economically, and environmentally.

4.1. Unraveling the Internet of Things (IoT)

Understanding the core concept of IoT is the first step. The term 'Internet of Things' might sound technical, but it simply refers to the network of digital objects embedded with hardware that can interact with the environment. IoT devices, connected to the internet, can relay and receive data providing profound insights. They act as our eyes and ears, transporting us to the granular level of urban operations that were previously opaque to city administrators and inhabitants.

Let's explore the key components of an IoT system:

- **Sensors**: Devices like thermometers, accelerometers, or cameras, among others, gather a plethora of data.

- **Connectivity**: IoT sensors use connectivity options like cellular network, satellites, Wi-Fi, and more to send gathered data to IoT gateways or the cloud.

- **Data Processing**: Data, once collected, is analyzed for patterns and correlations, forming a basis for decision-making.

- **User Interface**: Lastly, the condensed information is delivered to end-users via applications, alerts, or other methods, to take informed actions.

Now, let's delve into how IoT impacts various aspects of urban development.

4.2. Smart Infrastructure

By applying IoT to infrastructure, we can attain great strides in sustainability and efficiency. Using the data gathered from the embedded sensors, administrators can monitor infrastructure in real-time, react swiftly to damages, and perform predictive maintenance even before a malaise manifests itself. As such, life expectancy of infrastructure can be extended while ensuring optimal performance.

For example, sensors embedded in roads could measure traffic flow and detect potholes, allowing for proactive repairs. Similarly, smart lighting can reduce electricity consumption by dimming the light when no presence is detected, enhancing energy efficiency significantly.

4.3. Sustainable Utilities Management

IoT makes utility management more efficient, thereby improving sustainability. By monitoring energy and water usage, authorities are able to identify inefficiencies and thefts, helping reduce wastage of these precious resources.

Smart grids, with intelligent meters, provide real-time data about energy usage patterns. They also allow two-way communication enabling consumers to manage their consumption better, and save money, while the grid can auto-balance and handle faults more effectively.

Water management, aided by IoT, helps monitor water quality, detect leakages, and manage floods, profoundly impacting water conservation efforts.

4.4. Autonomous Transportation

Wireless vehicle-to-vehicle communication, supported by the IoT, makes transportation safer, faster, and more efficient. Traffic management systems can adjust signals based on current road conditions, reducing congestion and improving road safety. Connected vehicles can "talk" to each other and their surroundings, potentially evading accidents.

Autonomous or driverless cars, laced with IoT sensors, collect extensive data about their environment, navigating the path safely while reducing greenhouse gas emissions by optimizing fuel consumption.

4.5. Waste Management

IoT brings incredible changes to waste management practices. Smart bins fitted with sensors can alert the respective waste management agencies when they're full, ensuring timely and efficient waste collection. This helps in preventing overflows and reduces the time and costs involved in unnecessary collection rounds when bins are not full.

4.6. Public Safety and Security

The rise of IoT also escalates security by implementing smart surveillance systems utilizing advanced image recognition technologies. IoT-enabled emergency services equip firefighters, police, and medical personnel with real-time data on emergencies, paving the quickest and safest route to the site.

Predictive policing, aided by pattern analysis and AI, can preempt crime hotspots based on historical data, thus improving the safety of neighborhoods.

4.7. Citizen Engagement

IoT enabled smart city applications can provide residents insights about a gamut of affairs, such as air quality, noise levels, pollen count, and much more. They can compare energy consumption patterns and save costs, find empty parking spaces, locate nearby recycling centers, among various other services—enriching their lives and saving valuable time.

===Conclusion

The scale and scope of the IoT are extensive in urban development—it illuminates the dark corners of urban operations, uplifts the quality of services, heightens city management efficiency, and above all, nudges inhabitants and administrators towards a sustainable, green urban living.

Yet, this technological leap requires secure data management techniques and regulations, robust privacy safeguards, and strong cybersecurity measures. Stringent standards and protocols will have to be maintained to cater to unique challenges that advanced technologies like IoT present.

In the final analysis, the Internet of Things has dramatically transformed the prospects and paradigms of urban development. It connects the dots of an intricate urban network, pushing it towards efficiency, sustainability, and smartness, making the cities of tomorrow a reality of today. Unleashing the full potential of IoT acts as a keystone for our pursuit of smart, sustainable cities.

Chapter 5. Incorporating AI: Enhancing City Services

The fusion of Artificial Intelligence (AI) with city services is poised to revolutionize the way urban spaces function. From managing traffic to reducing waste, the promise of AI shines brilliantly across myriad spheres of city services.

5.1. The AI Landscape in City Services

AI's role in city services can be best understood by dividing it into two broad categories—automation and augmentation. Automation, unsurprisingly, is about taking tasks traditionally carried out by humans and automating them. Augmentation, on the other hand, takes tasks that humans already do and makes them vastly more efficient through the use of AI.

On the automation side, AI can take over a host of routine tasks that have traditionally required human intervention. For instance, scheduling public transportation, managing city utilities, and controlling traffic lights could all be entrusted to intelligent systems tuned to the rhythms of the city.

When it comes to augmentation, AI can elevate human decision-making to a whole new level by providing valuable insights and predictions. AI-based predictive analytics can aid in tackling crime, managing energy consumption, prepare for natural disasters, and much more.

5.2. Transportation and Traffic Management

One of the areas we are starting to see great improvements in through AI is transportation and traffic management. AI systems can analyze data from a myriad of sources like CCTV footage, social media posts, and GPS data to predict traffic patterns. Traffic management authorities can then use these insights to optimize traffic signals, identify congestion patterns, and effectively manage emergency situations.

Over time, AI algorithms can learn from the data and get better at predicting not only daily traffic fluctuations but more complex events such as the impact of a concert at a sports arena or the added pressure of tourists during the holidays.

Public transportation systems can also profit immensely from AI intervention. From optimizing routes based on ever-changing demand patterns to predicting maintenance needs, AI can make public transportation more reliable and efficient.

5.3. Public Safety and Emergency Services

AI can be a game-changer when it comes to public safety and emergency services. Fire departments, for example, are using AI to predict where fires are most likely to break out based on historical incident data and current weather conditions. This allows departments to strategically position resources, giving them a head start when fires do occur.

Similarly, predictive policing—where sophisticated AI systems analyze historical crime data to predict where crimes are likely to occur—is being explored. While it can be controversial, as it must be delicately balanced with civil rights, there is no denying its potential to make cities safer.

In the event of emergencies, AI's ability to analyze vast data sets in real-time can help triage incidents and allocate emergency services where they are most required. This will minimize response times and possibly save more lives in the process.

5.4. Waste Management

Waste management poses significant challenges to growing urban areas. Here too, AI has significant contributions to make. With the help of AI, waste collection routes can be optimized to reduce fuel consumption and costs.

Furthermore, AI can also assist in identifying waste patterns, determining the most likely times when bins will be full. This way, collection vehicles can avoid making unnecessary trips when the bins are not full, saving time and energy.

5.5. Energy Management and Conservation

AI can play a substantial role in energy management and conservation. By analyzing patterns in energy usage, AI systems can predict demand and ensure that supply is effectively managed to reduce waste.

For instance, AI algorithms running on smart grids could predict energy usage and delegate energy production accordingly, reducing the environmental impact. Similarly, energy consumption in public buildings can be optimized with AI-enabled systems, adjusting heating and cooling systems based on external temperature, occupancy, and time of day.

AI's capabilities extend to renewable energy sources as well. AI systems can predict wind speed and sunshine hours to optimize the output from wind and solar power plants. Additionally, AI can predict maintenance needs of these plants, improving their efficiency and lifespan.

5.6. Conclusion

The potential for AI to transform city services is vast and relatively untapped. From transportation and traffic management to public safety and waste management, AI can revolutionize how cities operate and make them more efficient, safe, and sustainable. Harnessing the power of AI is crucial for the successful development of smart cities. However, it is essential to balance this exploitation with considerations of privacy and ethical dimensions to truly turn the promise of AI into a reality for the betterment of our urban lives.

When properly managed, the convergence of AI and city services holds the vast potential to enhance efficiencies, save resources, and pave the way for a more sustainable and smarter city life. By continually learning and adapting, AI can provide solutions to many of the problems that plague cities today, turning them from urban jungles into smart habitats designed for optimal human living.

Chapter 6. Green Urban Planning and Development

The concept of green urban planning and development is not entirely new, but as we grapple with the challenges of climate change and urbanization, it has become increasingly significant. The core of this new wave of city planning is the synergy between urban development and the environment, creating urban habitats that are sustainable, livable, and efficient.

6.1. The Essence of Green Urban Planning

Green urban planning, or sustainable urban development, refers to the planning and design of cities, towns, and other urban areas to enhance sustainability. This includes careful management of resources, conservation of the natural environment, and the provision of a healthy living environment for residents. High-quality public infrastructure, renewable energy sources, efficient transportation, waste management, and efficient land use all contribute to realizing this ambitious vision.

At its core, green urban planning seeks to strike a balance between environmental, social, and economic sustainability, the so-called "triple bottom line" of sustainability. It emphasizes a long-term perspective, where the needs of the present are met without compromising the ability of future generations to meet their own needs.

6.2. Innovative Design and Land Use

Eco-design and efficient land use are vital elements of green urban planning, aimed at minimizing disruption to the environment while maximizing utilization of available resources. Whether it involves the allocation of space for parks and green zones, water and energy efficiency measures in buildings, or the layout and orientation of urban structures for optimal solar and wind usage, all these considerations factor into sustainable city design.

Furthermore, innovations such as green roofs and walls—structures that are covered in vegetation—contribute towards reducing urban heat island effect, improving air quality, and providing green spaces within dense urban environments.

6.3. Energy Efficiency and Renewable Energy

Energy sustainability is a key aspect of green urban planning. By using energy efficient design, technology, and construction methods, cities can significantly lower their energy consumption. Appropriate insulation, energy efficient appliances, and use of natural light via strategic building design are just a few examples.

At the same time, cities must shift from dependency on fossil fuels towards renewable energy sources like solar, wind, and geothermal. For instance, solar panels can be integrated into building designs or installed on rooftops, wind turbines can be placed in suitable urban and peri-urban locations, and the use of geothermal energy for heating and cooling can be explored.

Infrastructures such as district heating and cooling systems, energy recovery from waste, and decentralization of energy production systems can encourage the use of renewable energy and create resilient energy systems in cities.

6.4. Waste Management

Proper waste management is essential for urban sustainability. The goal should be to recycle as much waste as possible and minimize the amount sent to landfills. This requires planning for adequate recycling facilities, composting options for organic waste, as well as public education about recycling and waste minimization.

Moreover, the idea of a circular economy—where waste becomes a resource—can be integrated into urban planning. Concepts like industrial symbiosis, where the waste product of one industry becomes the input of another, and creating energy from waste, can significantly contribute to sustainable urban living.

6.5. Sustainable Transportation

Green urban planning needs to focus on both improving public transportation and encouraging non-motorized forms of transportation – walking and cycling. Prioritizing public transport can help reduce traffic congestion and lower carbon emissions, while bike lanes and pedestrian-friendly areas promote physical activity and improve health.

Embracing smart transportation technologies, such as electric vehicles, autonomous vehicles, and integrated transport management systems, can further reduce the environmental impact of urban transportation.

6.6. The Role of Technology in Green Urban Planning

Incorporating smart technology is key to achieving the goals of green urban planning. The use of big data and AI can optimize energy usage, waste management, and control transportation systems, while

Internet of Things (IoT) devices can provide valuable information to increase efficiency and conservation efforts.

Smart grids, which use digital communications technology to detect and react to local changes in usage, can improve the reliability, efficiency, and sustainability of urban energy.

6.7. Citizen Participation

Finally, residents play an important role in sustainable urban development, as their behaviour and lifestyle choices can significantly impact the sustainability of their city. Public education and involvement is therefore paramount, as is encouraging a sense of ownership and pride in the community's sustainability achievements.

The cities of tomorrow can be vibrant, thriving ecosystems that embrace progressive green urban planning without compromising the quality of urban life. Making the shift requires a total re-envisioning of how we plan, develop, and manage urban areas. Using green technologies innovatively and progressively is part of the roadmap to building these new-age urban spaces. It's an exciting future—and it all starts with sustainable foundations in green urban planning and development.

Chapter 7. Sustainable Energy Solutions for Smart Cities

The quest for sustainable energy solutions continues to shape the evolution of our earth's metropolises. For a city to be "smart", it must utilize digital technologies with the aim of enhancing performance and wellbeing, reducing costs and resource consumption, and engaging more effectively and actively with its citizens. Integral to this process is the adoption of sustainable energy strategies, which provide an environmentally-friendly alternative to traditional, nonrenewable energy sources, primarily fossil fuels.

7.1. What are sustainable Energy Solutions?

Sustainable energy solutions aim to meet the needs of the present without compromising the ability of future generations to meet their own needs. This involves the employment of renewable sources of energy such as solar, wind, hydroelectric, geothermal, and biomass. These sources have a much lower environmental impact than conventional energy technologies and are endlessly renewable.

7.2. Why Sustainable energy Solutions in Smart Cities?

Energy consumption and carbon emissions are major challenges facing urban environments today. Smart cities provide a platform for the integration of sustainable energy solutions to address these challenges. Smart grids allow for the integration of renewable energy sources, provide demand response capabilities, and improve grid reliability.

A transition from fossil-fuel-based power generation to renewables has several significant advantages for cities. Reduced greenhouse gas emissions can mitigate climate change impacts, while less local air pollution can result in healthier urban environments. From an economic perspective, it can drive job growth and stability in the renewable energy sector.

7.3. The Role of Solar Energy

Solar energy, harvested through photovoltaic (PV) panels, is one of the most developed renewable technologies in the world. In the case of smart cities, it can be used to power homes, street lights, and even electric vehicles. Smart grids can play a key role in accommodating solar energy by controlling and balancing the input and output of power. Rooftop solar panels can transform houses into standalone power plants, promoting energy independency.

Energy storage technologies, such as batteries, can also be coupled with solar panels to store excess energy generated during daylight hours. This energy can be used when solar energy generation is not possible, facilitating a continuous power supply.

7.4. Embracing Wind Energy

Wind turbines in and around cities can contribute significantly to their power supply. Winds are stronger and more constant on rooftops than at street level, making tall buildings streamlined for wind a potential source of power. While noise and vibration have been historically a hindrance, innovative technologies are overcoming these challenges, enabling quiet and non-vibrating wind turbines suitable for urban environments.

Wind energy complements solar power as it can often be harvested during periods when there is no sun. Thus, the combination of wind and solar energy can provide a more constant and stable supply of power.

7.5. The Promise of Hydroelectric Power

Even though traditionally associated with large infrastructure projects, hydroelectric power also holds potential for urban areas. Small-scale hydro power projects can provide electricity for individual buildings or city districts. Kinetic energy can be harvested from moving water in rivers and canals or even wastewater in city pipes, providing a non-stop power source with little environmental impact.

7.6. Geothermal Energy and Heat Pumps

Geothermal offers yet another sustainable way of heating and cooling buildings. This technology harnesses heat from the earth or groundwater, depending on local conditions. Even district heating and cooling can benefit from geothermal sources. Given that heating and cooling typically account for a large proportion of a city's energy consumption, geothermal can notably improve a city's energy efficiency.

7.7. Biomass Energy

Biomass, organic material coming from plants and animals, can also contribute to the sustainable energy mix of a city. Waste-to-energy plants transform municipal solid waste into heat and electricity, thus dealing simultaneously with waste management and power generation.

7.8. The Future of Sustainable Energy in Smart Cities

The future of sustainable energy in smart cities is promising. Enormous technological strides are being made in renewable energy sources and their integration into urban systems. The smart city of the future is likely to have a sophisticated, diversified, and sustainable energy system that uses a mix of different technologies, suited to specific local conditions.

Even more than the technologies themselves, the real transformative power comes from new ways of thinking about energy: not as a commodity, but as a shared resource; not as a cost, but an investment in our future; not as a problem, but a solution to our environmental challenges. This paradigm shift - driven by technology - has the potential to change not only our cities but our world as well.

As more and more cities embrace the 'smart' revolution, it is important to keep sustainability at the forefront. The development of sustainable energy solutions is not only a response to our global environmental challenges, but also a step towards enhancing the quality of urban life and creating more prosperous, resilient cities.

Chapter 8. Intelligent Transportation: Mobility in the Smart City

Urban living comes with a host of advantages: convenience, opportunity, a bustling network of communities—however, it also brings a set of challenges to the table, critical among these being transportation. Currently, traditional urban transport systems are facing numerous burdens, from congestion to pollution to inadequate infrastructure. As we look towards building cities of the future—Smart Cities, we must reevaluate these challenges and find effective, sustainable solutions.

Advancements in technology present us with an opportunity to fundamentally reimagine urban mobility from the ground up. By marrying technological innovation with sustainable practices, we're inching closer to creating Intelligent Transportation Systems (ITS) that prioritize efficiency, efficacy, and eco-friendliness.

8.1. ITS: An Overview

Intelligent Transport Systems (ITS) employ technology, communications, data processing, and control systems to improve the safety, effectiveness, and environmental sustainability of transportation networks. They work to reduce traffic congestion, improve road safety, enhance the efficiency of public transportation, and reduce carbon emissions—overall, offering a more integrated, user-friendly way of traveling.

Significant elements of an intelligent transportation system include traffic management systems, public transport management, travel information systems, active modes of travel, environmental monitoring, and fleet management. Each of these elements, individually and collectively, can impact the livability, productivity, and sustainability of a city.

8.2. Traffic Management Systems

Traffic management systems are the backbone of an intelligent transportation system. Advances in technologies like AI and IoT (Internet of Things) enable real-time monitoring, analysis, and control of traffic flow. With predictive modeling and adaptive traffic signal control systems, traffic congestion can be significantly reduced, enhancing road capacity. Countless hours previously wasted stuck in traffic can be put to productive use, while also significantly reducing pollution caused by idling vehicles.

8.3. Public Transport Management

Efficient public transportation is the key to a truly smart city. With a combination of technologies like GPS, IoT, Machine Learning and Cloud Computing, public transport can be optimized like never before. Real-time information, such as arrival times, seat availability, and traffic situations, can be communicated to commuters, enabling them to plan their commutes more effectively. Meanwhile, transport providers can use data analytics to monitor their fleets continuously and ensure maximum efficiency.

8.4. Travel Information Systems

An effective travel information system allows residents and visitors to gain real-time information about their journey. By harnessing the power of mobile applications, and in-car systems, users can have access to information on traffic, weather, parking, detours, and the most fuel-efficient routes. This significantly improves the overall experience of commuting.

8.5. Active Modes of Travel

Promoting active travel modes like cycling and walking can significantly reduce the environmental footprint of a city while promoting healthier lifestyles among its citizens. Smart city platforms can facilitate active modes through features such as interactive maps for safe walking and cycling paths, bike-sharing schemes, and real-time weather information.

8.6. Environmental Monitoring

Environmental monitoring is another vital component of intelligent transport systems. Sensors installed throughout the city can monitor air quality, noise levels, and other environmental parameters. This data can be used to develop strategic plans and policy decisions aimed at reducing the environmental impact of transport.

8.7. Fleet Management

Efficient fleet management is integral to the functioning of service-based industries such as public transportation, logistics, and rental services. Technologies like telematics, GPS, and real-time analytics can help manage and track the fleet, ensuring optimal route planning, reducing fuel consumption and minimizing downtime.

In conclusion, Intelligent Transport Systems are the way forward for cities to ensure efficient and sustainable urban mobility. As we leverage technological advancements, we must also keep environmental considerations at the forefront. By doing so, we can ensure that our future cities are not just smart, but also sustainable. From reducing congestion to promoting active modes of transport—the potential for innovation is immense and remains a central theme to the evolution of smarter cities. We must be open to experimentation, learn from each iteration, and continuously work towards the betterment of our cities.

As we envision the future, technological advancements cannot replace the need for planning and policy implementation—they must go hand in hand. Technology provides us with the tools to make informed decisions; however, the onus is on us to make those decisions wisely and sustainably. Our journey to the cities of tomorrow is an ongoing process, one that requires the collective effort of all stakeholders—policymakers, city planners, industry leaders, and most importantly, the community. We must all, collectively, work towards creating cities that are not just efficient and smart but are also sustainable and inclusive. The road to the future is a shared journey—let's ensure it's a smart and sustainable one!

Chapter 9. Digital Governance: Streamlining City Administration

In an era characterized by rapid digital transformation, leveraging technology for efficient administration is a must. City governance isn't left behind in this exciting journey. So what does Digital Governance mean in the context of Smart Cities, and how is it breathing life into the administration?

Digital governance involves the application of digital tools and methods to governing functions and activities, enhancing efficiencies, transparency, and effectiveness—a shift from traditional bureaucratic methods to an agile, data-driven, digital-first approach. While it may sound complex, it becomes straightforward when broken down to individual components. In the context of Smart Cities, it encompasses three essential aspects: e-government initiatives, data management, and digital equity.

9.1. E-Government Initiatives

Increasingly, governments are deploying digital solutions aimed at simplifying processes and making them more accessible. Such initiatives significantly influence public services by streamlining them, saving time and resources. This eliminates paperwork, simplifying the on-boarding of services, and reducing administrative overheads. Additionally, e-government employs data-driven decision-making, which results in better planning and policies.

A perfect embodiment of an effective e-government initiative is Estonia's e-Residency program. It enables global citizens to start and manage a business online under Estonia's advanced digital infrastructure, boosting the country's economy and transforming it into a digital society. While this is a national level implementation, it can be a model for city administrations, particularly for those focusing on improving business conditions and attracting investments.

9.2. Data Management

Cities are treasure troves of data, which if utilized effectively, can direct policymaking towards the real needs of the community, drive operational efficiencies, and help in proactive rather than reactive decision-making.

Handling city data, however, is a colossal task ideated on a foundation of robust data management plans, comprising data collection, storage, analysis, and security. Many cities, like Chicago with its "WindyGrid" platform, develop real-time geospatial data systems that integrate various city data to gain insights for better decision-making and to anticipate problems before they become critical.

Critical to the success of such initiatives is the focus on data security and privacy. Administration by nature handles sensitive personal information; hence ensuring it remains safe and is used ethically is paramount.

9.3. Digital Equity

In the quest for digital transformation, it is vital to ensure that everyone has equal access to digital resources—this is digital equity. Gaps in access to technologies can spread inequalities and impede residents from participating fully in the digital city. Thus, initiatives should be aimed at providing affordable Internet access, digital literacy training, and easy access to digital services.

Seattle is a leader in promoting digital equity, with initiatives like the

Technology Matching Fund, which grants funds to organizations working towards increasing access to technology and providing digital skills training among underserved communities.

While we visualize a technologically advanced future, multiple challenges lie ahead. Transforming into a digitally governed city isn't effortless and instantaneous. It requires an adaptive institutional culture, investment in digital infrastructure, extensive training for city staff, and continuous commitment to digital equity. Ultimately, the goal is to leverage technology to enhance the quality of life and wellbeing of every citizen.

As they say, "The best way to predict the future is to build it." By imbibing digital governance into city administration, we can take a significant step towards that endeavor. In essence, digital governance in the framework of smart cities signifies a future wherein technology is not a mere enabler but an active participant in shaping an inclusive, sustainable, and equitable urban world.

Chapter 10. Citizen Engagement in the Age of Smart Cities

In comprehending the evolution of cities into their smarter versions, the key ingredient that necessitates attention is undoubtedly the citizens themselves. The transition from mere inhabitants to proactive individuals contributing to urban evolution forms the core base of our study. As the name suggests, Smart Cities aren't solely about the amalgamation of tech-savvy infrastructure; they rely much on the participation and interaction of citizens making conscious, intelligent decisions in their everyday lives.

10.1. The Elevation of Citizen Engagement: A Paradigm Shift

Today's era, earmarked by the robust use of digital technology, has instigated a significant shift in how citizens engage with their cities. From the traditional passive receipt of public services, we now witness an era where individuals turn into active contributors towards developing their living spaces. This change—a pivot from a controlled administration to a shared co-creation of urban spaces—offers not only incredible opportunities for innovation and sustainability but also challenges to effective citizen engagement.

An efficient citizen engagement system renders the citizens no longer just consumers, but producers of services, forming a clear symbiosis of collective responsibility towards the city's growth and sustainability. This engagement brings about a fundamental change, making cities posited to not just 'adapt' smart technology in infrastructure but also in 'decision making', 'planning' and 'sustainability' aspects—an all-around smart city.

10.2. Digital Democracy and Citizen Participation

With the advent of the internet, the traditional barriers to citizen participation, such as time and location constraints, are blurring. Citizens can now actively participate in city governance from the comfort of their homes. From online opinion pooling to e-voting, the internet has democratized participation, well beyond just access to information. It's evolving into a powerful tool for collaboration, cooperation, and co-creation, paving the way for digital democracy.

Artificial Intelligence (AI) platforms, with their vast computing capabilities, are being harnessed for public sentiment analysis, helping in understanding citizen views on specific initiatives and policies. E-governance portals, smart apps, and chatbots provide intuitive platforms for citizens to voice their concerns, pitch constructive ideas, and report local issues—thus being indispensable tools for citizen engagement.

10.3. Citizen Science and the Internet of Things (IoT)

The rapid growth of IoT enables an innovative facet of citizen engagement—Citizen Science. Here, citizens become the sensors themselves, collecting and sharing local data around them. The proliferation of smartphones and wearable devices enables this, making every citizen a potential data collector, contributing to the city's 'big data' pool. This data helps in making neighbourhood-specific decisions, leading to truly decentralized and pragmatic urban planning.

Collection of microclimate data, traffic patterns, air and noise pollution levels, become more precise with citizen participation. Moreover, this active engagement not only aids in data gathering but helps forge a stronger bond between the citizen and the city—making the citizen more conscious and motivated towards sustainable, smart living.

10.4. Ensuring Inclusivity in Citizen Engagement

While technology plays a pioneering role in citizen engagement, it's vital to ensure inclusivity. The digital divide, especially concerning older adults and residents from underprivileged communities, can become a significant obstacle if not addressed deliberately. Hence, initiatives should aim at bridging this gap—through continuous education, simpler UX/UI, and creating offline touchpoints in critical areas.

In addition, 'Participative Budgeting' can prove to be another inclusion strategy, where citizens have their say directly in the allocation of certain parts of the municipal budget. Such approaches ensure citizen-centric developmental plans and give rise to cities that resonate with the real needs and aspirations of their citizens.

10.5. Citizen Engagement for Sustainability

Citizen engagement, when well-utilized, can act as a strong stimulator towards building sustainable cities. Smart meters, for instance, provide real-time energy consumption data to the users, building awareness and promoting behaviour change towards more sustainable energy usage. Climate apps help citizens plan their day with the least carbon footprint, encouraging green living.

Equally crucial is creating a platform where citizens and city administration can actively join hands to devise and implement green initiatives. Working together creates a sense of collective ownership and responsibility, fostering an overall sustainable climate in the city.

To summarize, citizen engagement in the age of smart cities isn't simply a nice-to-have, it is a cornerstone upon which the success of these futuristic urban paradises rests. It's the harnessing of the collective power of the citizens that will ensure urban ecosystems evolve in a way that's sustainable, smart, and, most importantly, inclusive. This unique intersection of technology, democracy, and sustainability provides a refreshing perspective on how we can collectively build our cities of tomorrow. After all, a smart city is as smart as its citizens.

Chapter 11. Walking the Tightrope: Balancing Technology and Privacy

In light of the remarkable rise in sophisticated technology, cities across the globe are harnessing the benefits to optimize urban living—becoming "smarter." Yet, this rapid digital advancement presents a delicate balancing act between progress and privacy. To fully appreciate this dynamic, we'll journey through the intricate labyrinth of data handling, surveillance, protection laws, public awareness, acceptance, and structured guidelines necessary to secure the private sphere.

11.1. Defining the Borders: Privacy in a Digital Age

The concept of 'privacy' has notoriously been a nebulous matter, often subjective and varying significantly among cultures, individuals and the evolving zeitgeist. Today's understanding of privacy in the digital age encapsulates the right to control who accesses one's personal information and under what conditions. This conception of privacy stands challenged in an increasingly connected ecosystem humming with data transactions that form the backbone of a Smart City.

Smart Cities aggregate vast amounts of data, collected from IoT devices, sensor networks, and citizen's digital footprints. This data is analyzed and translated into efficient and personalized public services. However, this level of intrusive data collection and processing has raised justified concerns over the potential misuse of personal information, leading to a rousing discourse on the balance of technology and privacy.

11.2. Under Watchful Eyes: Surveillance in Smart Cities

As technology propels us into a future dominated by artificial intelligence, machine learning and hyper-connectivity, cities are employing smarter systems to streamline urban living. A significant aspect of this involves constant data collection. Eyes perched atop buildings, smart traffic management systems, and even tools designed to forecast crimes before they occur, have blurred the line between protection and intrusion.

Citizens are often oblivious to the depth of surveillance that has seeped subtly into their daily lives. As public spaces brim with smart technologies geared towards creating secure and lively environments, the trade-off between urban efficiency, safety provisions, and the resultant intrusion into the residents' privacy becomes a contentious issue that demands urgent attention and appropriate regulation.

11.3. Passing the Act: A Look at Privacy Laws

Across jurisdictions, privacy laws are often fragmented and lack the robustness needed to guard against the rampant rise of data breaches. Regulation such as the European Union's General Data Protection Regulation (GDPR) sets the global benchmark. Grounded on principles like fairness, transparency, accuracy, and data minimization, laws like the GDPR safeguard user privacy, establish users' rights over their data, and ensure that data processing aligns with the intended purpose.

Yet, many regions lag behind the GDPR standards and are yet to catch up to these comprehensive legal frameworks. This piecemeal progress suggests that the years ahead must focus on global synchronization and upgrading of data protection standards.

11.4. Technology as a Guardian: Privacy by Design

As paradoxical as it may appear, technology itself could emerge as the knight on white on this chessboard. The 'Privacy by Design' principle emphasizes embedding privacy measures into the design of a system or a product from the onset, instead of it being an afterthought.

It's a promising solution that uses encryption, anonymization, and pseudonymization as shields against unauthorized incursions, ensuring limited data processing, safe storage, secure communication channels, and the secure disposal of surplus data. Further advancements in technology shall birth new tools to bolster this saga of privacy protection.

11.5. Wiser Public: Privacy Awareness and Acceptance

The complexity of technology and its profound integration in our lives often leaves the average city dweller unaware of the overreach. As the beating heart of Smart Cities, citizens need to be equipped with the knowledge of the technology that surrounds them and the potential implications on their privacy. Public awareness drives should be a part of the Smart City blueprint, incentivizing citizen vigilance.

Simultaneously, acceptance plays an instrumental role in the discourse. Some degree of privacy surrender is inevitable and could be acceptable for personalized, efficient services. However, it must hinge on informed consent, where users are aware of the extent, purpose of data collection, and hold the right to withdraw it.

11.6. Ebbing Waves: Structured Guidelines for Smart Cities

The development of Smart City guidelines is imperative to create and maintain the delicate balance of privacy and technology. These guidelines should revolve around the ethical collection, storage, processing, sharing, and disposing of data. They should also dictate the protocol during security breaches, ensuring transparency towards the victims and robust actions to prevent further damage.

The journey towards smart sustainability involves a heightened reliance on technology. As cities transform and adapt to these digital shifts, the concerns around privacy will continue to occupy a central position. The task ahead is in striking the right balance, allowing progress but not at the cost of citizens' privacy, making cities not just smarter, but safer. As we wade into this new digital era, it is crucial that our rights evolve and grow with it, serving as our compass guiding our steps into the technologically vibrant and privacy-respecting Smart Cities of tomorrow.

www.ingramcontent.com/pod-product-compliance
Lightning Source LLC
Chambersburg PA
CBHW071034260726
48661CB00007B/3023